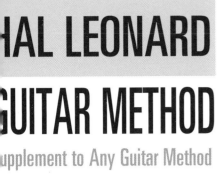

HAL LEONARD
GUITAR METHOD

Supplement to Any Guitar Method

EASY POP MELODIES
THIRD EDITION

INTRODUCTION

Welcome to *Easy Pop Melodies*, a collection of 20 pop and rock favorites arranged for easy guitar. If you're a beginning guitarist, you've come to the right place; these well-known songs will have you playing, reading, and enjoying music in no time!

This book can be used on its own or as a supplement to the *Hal Leonard Guitar Method* or any other beginning guitar method. The songs are arranged in order of difficulty. Each melody is presented in an easy-to-read format—including lyrics to help you follow along and chords for optional accompaniment (by your teacher, if you have one).

ISBN 978-0-7935-7385-1

HAL•LEONARD®
7777 W. BLUEMOUND RD. P.O. BOX 13819 MILWAUKEE, WI 53213

Visit Hal Leonard Online at
www.halleonard.com

SONG STRUCTURE

The songs in this book have different sections, which may or may not include the following:

Intro
This is usually a short instrumental section that "introduces" the song at the beginning.

Verse
This is one of the main sections of a song and conveys most of the storyline. A song usually has several verses, all with the same music but each with different lyrics.

Chorus
This is often the most memorable section of a song. Unlike the verse, the chorus usually has the same lyrics every time it repeats.

Bridge
This section is a break from the rest of the song, often having a very different chord progression and feel.

Solo
This is an instrumental section, often played over the verse or chorus structure.

Outro
Similar to an intro, this section brings the song to an end.

ENDINGS & REPEATS

Many of the songs have some new symbols that you must understand before playing. Each of these represents a different type of ending.

1st and 2nd Endings
These are indicated by brackets and numbers. The first time through a song section, play the first ending and then repeat. The second time through, skip the first ending, and play through the second ending.

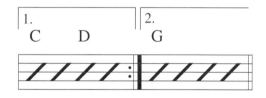

D.S.
This means "Dal Segno" or "from the sign." When you see this abbreviation above the staff, find the sign (𝄋) earlier in the song and resume playing from that point.

al Coda
This means "to the Coda," a concluding section in the song. If you see the words "D.S. al Coda," return to the sign (𝄋) earlier in the song and play until you see the words "To Coda," then skip to the Coda at the end of the song, indicated by the symbol: ⊕.

al Fine
This means "to the end." If you see the words "D.S. al Fine," return to the sign (𝄋) earlier in the song and play until you see the word "Fine."

D.C.
This means "Da Capo" or "from the head." When you see this abbreviation above the staff, return to the beginning (or "head") of the song and resume playing.

CONTENTS

Can You Feel the Love Tonight
from THE LION KING

Music by Elton John
Words by Tim Rice

Verse

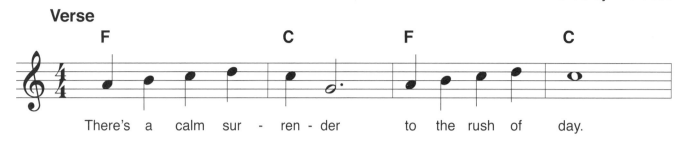

There's a calm sur - ren - der to the rush of day.

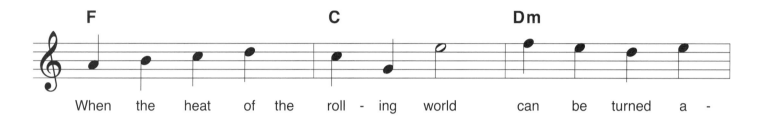

When the heat of the roll - ing world can be turned a -

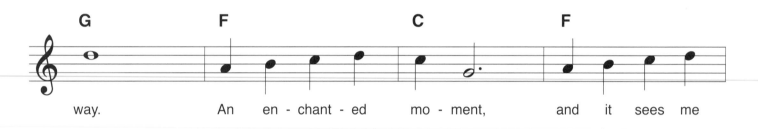

way. An en - chant - ed mo - ment, and it sees me

through. It's e - nough for this rest - less war - rior

Chorus

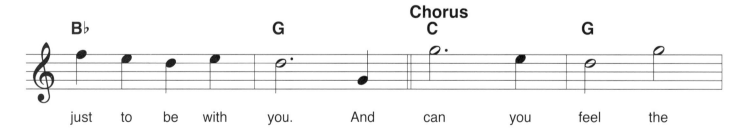

just to be with you. And can you feel the

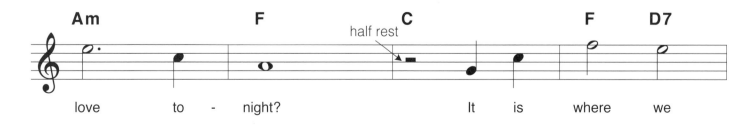

love to - night? It is where we

MY HEART WILL GO ON
(Love Theme from 'Titanic')
from the Paramount and Twentieth Century Fox Motion Picture TITANIC

Music by James Horner
Lyric by Will Jennings

Verse

1. Ev - 'ry night in my dreams I see you, I
2. Love can touch us one time and last for a

feel you. That is how I know you go
life - time, and nev - er let go you till we're

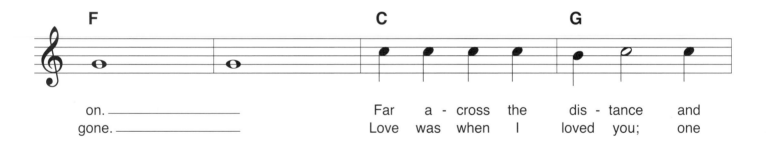

on. _____ Far a - cross the dis - tance and
gone. _____ Love was when I loved you; one

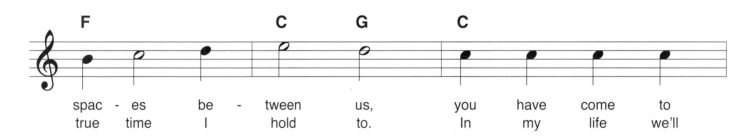

spac - es be - tween us, you have come to
true time I hold to. In my life we'll

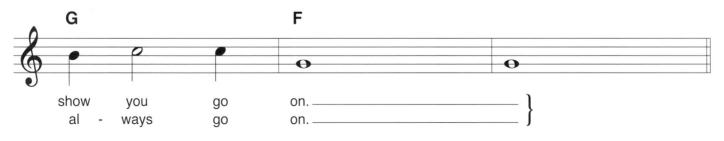

show you go on. _____
al - ways go on. _____

LET IT BE

Words and Music by
John Lennon and Paul McCartney

Verse

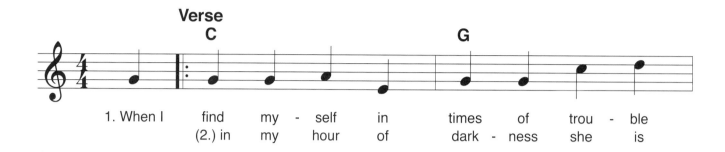

1. When I find my-self in times of trou - ble
(2.) in my hour of dark - ness she is

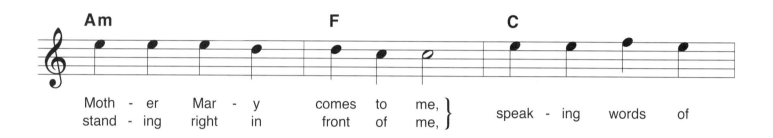

Moth - er Mar - y comes to me, }
stand - ing right in front of me, } speak - ing words of

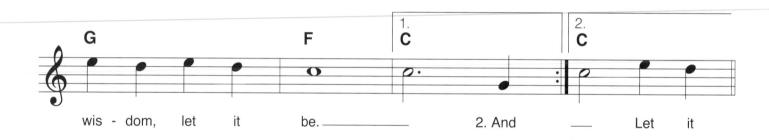

wis - dom, let it be. ____ 2. And ____ Let it

Chorus

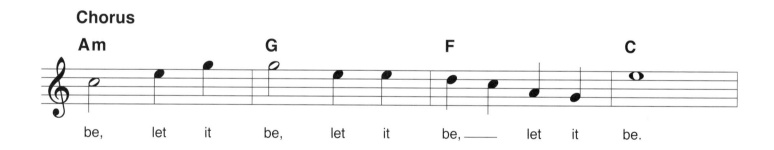

be, let it be, let it be, ____ let it be.

Whis - per words of wis - dom, let it be. ____

HEY THERE DELILAH

Words and Music by
Tom Higgenson

YOUR CHEATIN' HEART

Words and Music by
Hank Williams

All My Loving

Words and Music by
John Lennon and Paul McCartney

Verse

Close your eyes and I'll kiss you; to - mor - row I'll

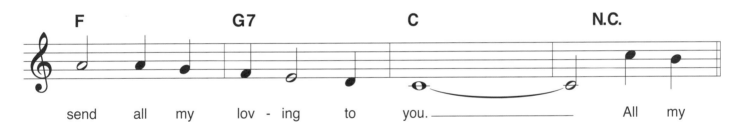

miss you. Re - mem - ber I'll al - ways be true. ___ And then

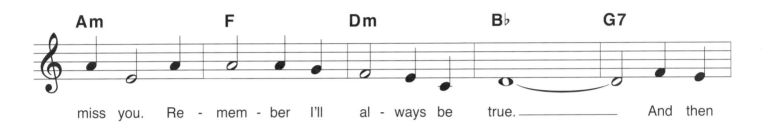

while I'm a - way, I'll write home ev - 'ry day. ___ I'll

send all my lov - ing to you. ___ All my

Chorus

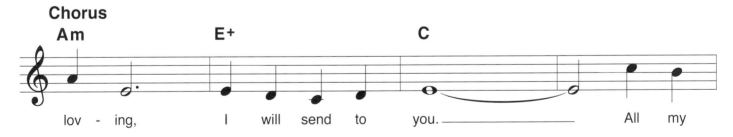

lov - ing, I will send to you. ___ All my

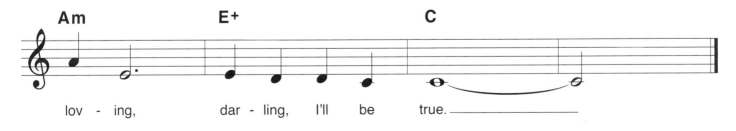

lov - ing, dar - ling, I'll be true. ___

LOVE ME TENDER

Words and Music by
Elvis Presley and Vera Matson

Verse

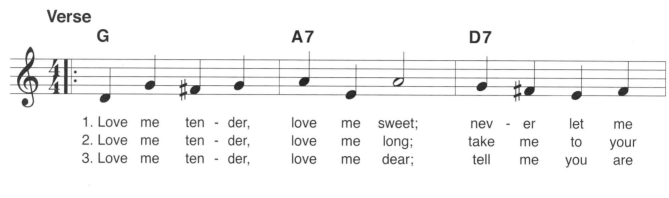

1. Love me ten - der, love me sweet; nev - er let me
2. Love me ten - der, love me long; take me to your
3. Love me ten - der, love me dear; tell me you are

go.   You have made my life com - plete, and I love you
heart.   For it's there that I be - long, and we'll nev - er
mine.   I'll be yours through all the years, till the end of

Chorus

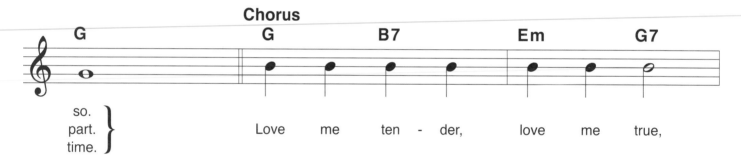

so.
part.
time.   Love me ten - der, love me true,

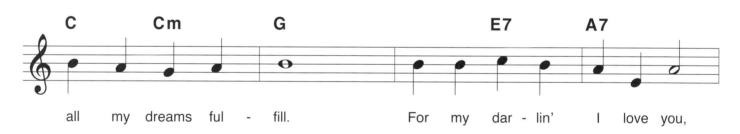

all my dreams ful - fill.   For my dar - lin' I love you,

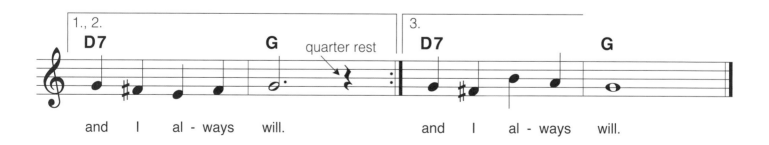

and I al - ways will.   and I al - ways will.

STAND BY ME

Words and Music by
Jerry Leiber, Mike Stoller and Ben E. King

GOOD RIDDANCE
(Time of Your Life)

Words by Billie Joe
Music by Green Day

Verse

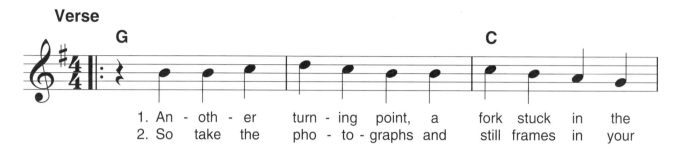

1. An - oth - er turn - ing point, a fork stuck in the
2. So take the pho - to - graphs and still frames in your

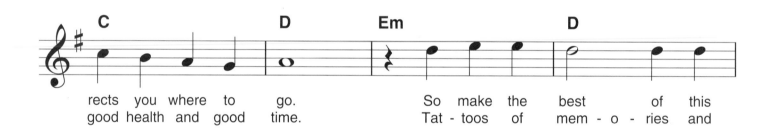

road.
mind.

Time grabs you by the wrist, di -
Hang it by on a shelf in

rects you where to go.
good health and good time.

So make the best of this
Tat - toos of mem - o - ries and

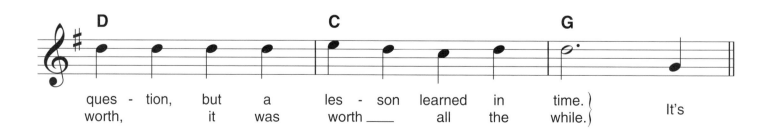

test and don't ask why. ____
dead ____ skin on trial. ____

It's not a
For what it's

ques - tion, but a les - son learned in time. }
worth, it was worth ____ all the while. }

It's

Chorus

some - ting   un - pre - dict - a - able,   but   in   the   end   is

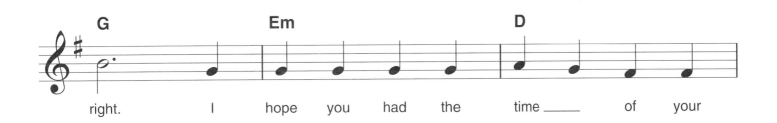

right.   I   hope   you   had   the   time _____ of   your

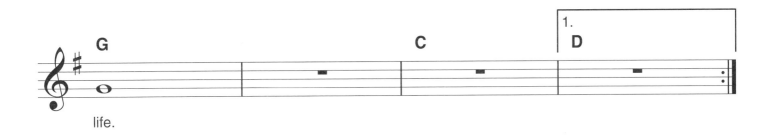

life.

It's   some - thing   un - pre - dict - a - ble,   but

in   the   end   is   right.   I   hope   you   had   the

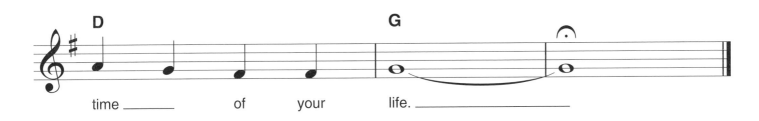

time _____ of   your   life. _____

I Walk the Line

Words and Music by
John R. Cash

key of G

※ **Verse**

D7

1. I keep a close watch on this heart of
(3.) night is on dark and day is

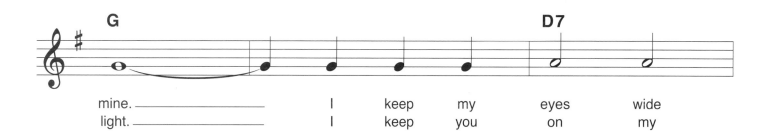

G   D7

mine. _____ I keep my eyes wide
light. _____ I keep you on my

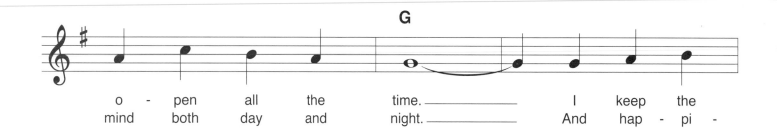

G

o - pen all the time. _____ I keep the
mind both day and night. _____ And hap - pi -

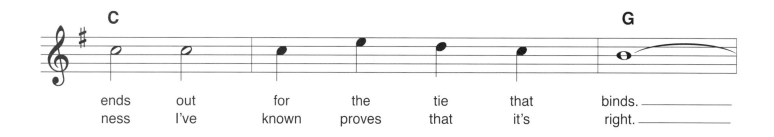

C   G

ends out for the tie that binds. _____
ness I've known the proves that it's right. _____

To Coda ✛

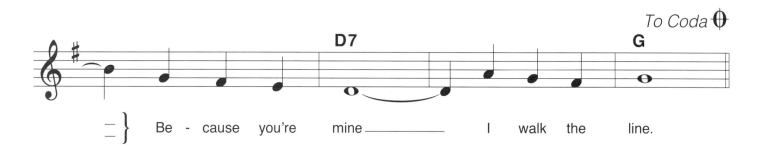

D7   G

Be - cause you're mine _____ I walk the line.

NOWHERE MAN

Words and Music by
John Lennon and Paul McCartney

Chorus

He's a real no - where man, sit - ting in his

no - where land, mak - ing all his no - where plans for

Verse

To Coda

no - bod - y. _____
1. Does - n't have a point of view,
2. He's as blind as he can be,

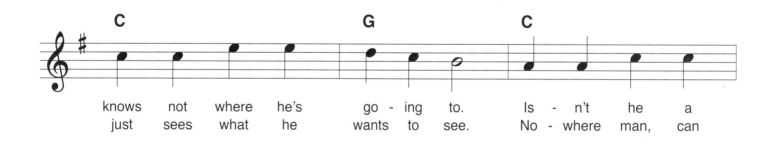

knows not where he's go - ing to. Is - n't he a
just sees what he wants to see. No - where man, can

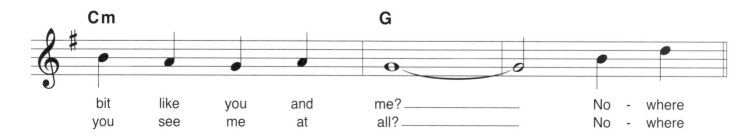

bit like you and me? _____ No - where
you see me at all? _____ No - where

Bridge

man, please lis - ten. You don't know what you're
man, don't wor - ry. Take your time, _____ don't

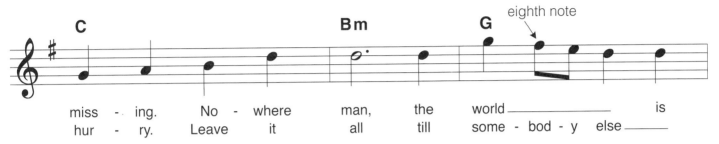

eighth note

miss - . ing. No - where man, the world _____ is
hur - ry. Leave it all till some - bod - y else _____

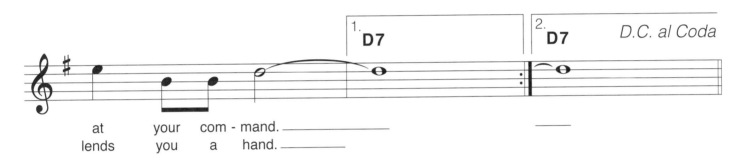

1. **D7** 2. **D7** *D.C. al Coda*

at your com - mand. _____
lends you a hand. _____

Coda

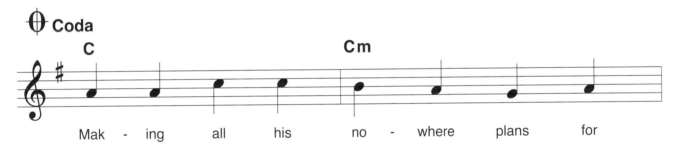

Mak - ing all his no - where plans for

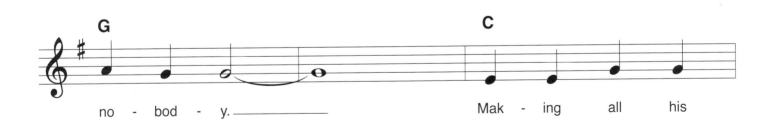

no - bod - y. _____ Mak - ing all his

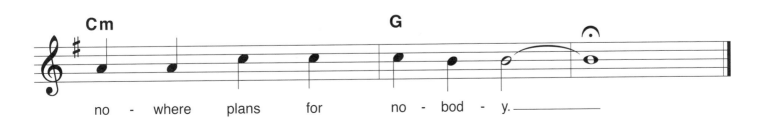

no - where plans for no - bod - y. _____

EVERY BREATH YOU TAKE

Music and Lyrics by
Sting

WE WILL ROCK YOU

Words and Music by
Brian May

21

DUST IN THE WIND

Words and Music by
Kerry Livgren

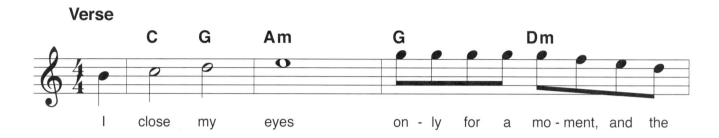

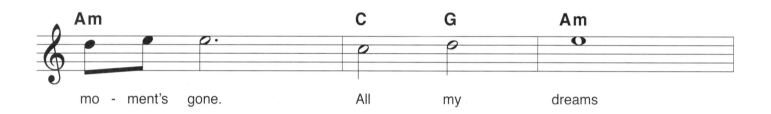

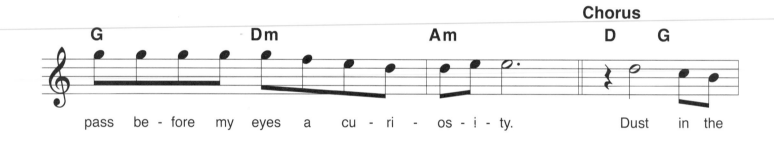

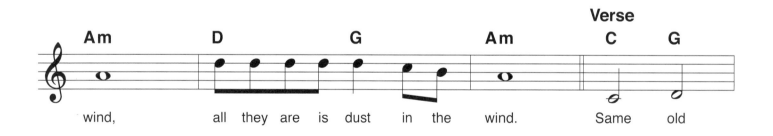

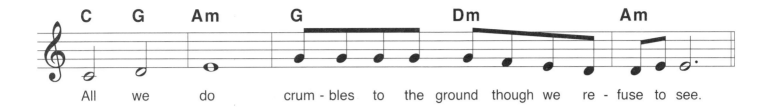

All we do crum-bles to the ground though we re-fuse to see.

Chorus

Dust in the wind, all we are is dust in the wind.

Verse

Don't hang on, noth-ing lasts for-ev-er but the earth and sky. It

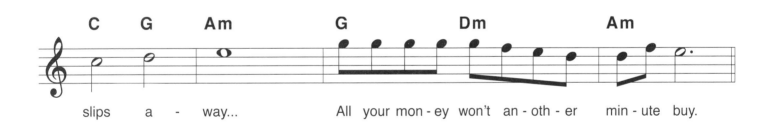

slips a - way... All your mon-ey won't an-oth-er min-ute buy.

Chorus

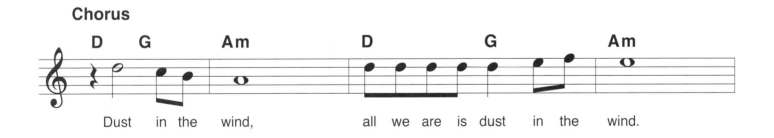

Dust in the wind, all we are is dust in the wind.

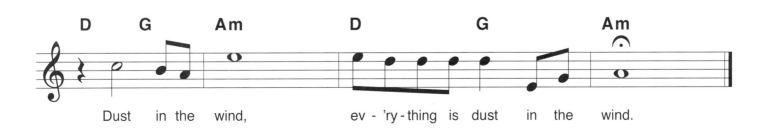

Dust in the wind, ev-'ry-thing is dust in the wind.

IMAGINE

Words and Music by
John Lennon

die for   and no re - li - gion too. ____

hun - ger,   a broth - er - hood of man. ____

Im - ag - ine all the peo - ple   liv - ing life in

Im - ag - ine all the peo - ple   shar - ing all the

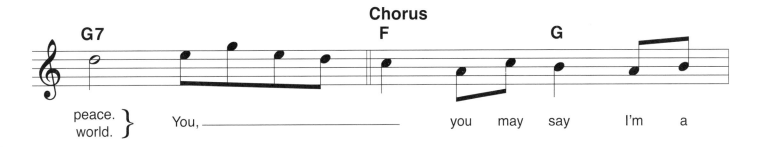

peace. / world.   You, _____ you may say I'm a

dream - er,   but I'm not the on - ly one.

I hope some day ____ you'll join ____ us

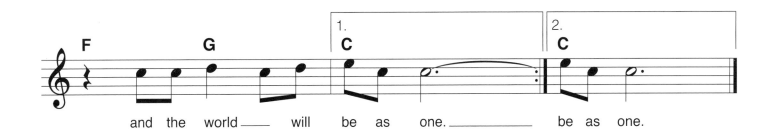

and the world ___ will be as one. ____ be as one.

MY CHERIE AMOUR

Words and Music by
Stevie Wonder, Sylvia Moy and Henry Cosby

I SHOT THE SHERIFF

Words and Music by
Bob Marley

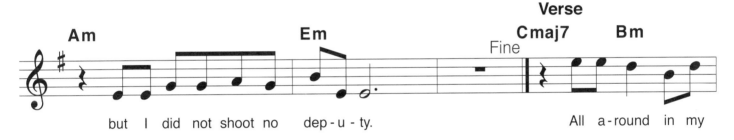

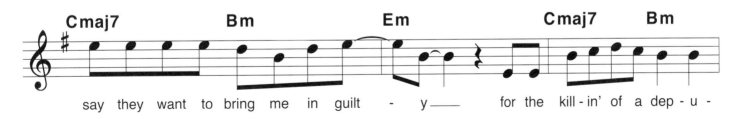

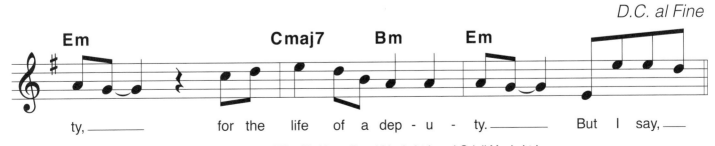

I GET AROUND

Words and Music by
Brian Wilson and Mike Love

D.S. al Coda

bud - dies and me ⸺ are get - tin' real well - known. ⸺ Yeah, the
guys go stead - y 'cause it wouldn't be right ⸺ to leave their

bad guys know us and they leave us a - lone. ⸺ } I get a
best girl home on a Sat - ur - day night. ⸺ }

Coda
G7   C
— Round, round, get a - round,

A7   Dm   B♭   G7
I get a - round. ⸺ Get a - round, woo - ooh, I get a - round. ⸺

Outro
C   A7
Get a - round, round, round, I get a - round. ⸺ Get a - round, round, round,

Dm
I get a - round. ⸺ Get a - round, round, round, I get a - round. ⸺

Repeat and fade
B♭   G7
Get a - round, round, round, I get a - round. ⸺

29

WALK DON'T RUN

By Johnny Smith

Smells Like Teen Spirit

Words and Music by
Kurt Cobain, Krist Novoselic and David Grohl

HAL LEONARD GUITAR METHOD

METHOD BOOKS, SONGBOOKS AND REFERENCE BOOKS

THE HAL LEONARD GUITAR METHOD is designed for anyone just learning to play acoustic or electric guitar. It is based on years of teaching guitar students of all ages, and it also reflects some of the best guitar teaching ideas from around the world. This comprehensive method includes: A learning sequence carefully paced with clear instructions; popular songs which increase the incentive to learn to play; versatility – can be used as self-instruction or with a teacher; audio accompaniments so that students have fun and sound great while practicing.

BOOK 1
00699010	Book Only	$8.99
00699027	Book/Online Audio	$12.99
00697341	Book/Online Audio + DVD	$24.99
00697318	DVD Only	$19.99
00155480	Deluxe Beginner Edition (Book, CD, DVD, Online Audio/ Video & Chord Poster)	$19.99

COMPLETE (BOOKS 1, 2 & 3)
00699040	Book Only	$16.99
00697342	Book/Online Audio	$24.99

BOOK 2
00699020	Book Only	$8.99
00697313	Book/Online Audio	$12.99

BOOK 3
00699030	Book Only	$8.99
00697316	Book/Online Audio	$12.99

Prices, contents and availability subject to change without notice.

STYLISTIC METHODS

ACOUSTIC GUITAR
00697347	Method Book/Online Audio	$17.99
00237969	Songbook/Online Audio	$16.99

BLUEGRASS GUITAR
00697405	Method Book/Online Audio	$16.99

BLUES GUITAR
00697326	Method Book/Online Audio (9" x 12")	$16.99
00697344	Method Book/Online Audio (6" x 9")	$15.99
00697385	Songbook/Online Audio (9" x 12")	$14.99
00248636	Kids Method Book/Online Audio	$12.99

BRAZILIAN GUITAR
00697415	Method Book/Online Audio	$17.99

CHRISTIAN GUITAR
00695947	Method Book/Online Audio	$16.99
00697408	Songbook/CD Pack	$14.99

CLASSICAL GUITAR
00697376	Method Book/Online Audio	$15.99

COUNTRY GUITAR
00697337	Method Book/Online Audio	$22.99
00697400	Songbook/Online Audio	$19.99

FINGERSTYLE GUITAR
00697378	Method Book/Online Audio	$21.99
00697432	Songbook/Online Audio	$16.99

FLAMENCO GUITAR
00697363	Method Book/Online Audio	$15.99

FOLK GUITAR
00697414	Method Book/Online Audio	$16.99

JAZZ GUITAR
00695359	Book/Online Audio	$22.99
00697386	Songbook/Online Audio	$15.99

JAZZ-ROCK FUSION
00697387	Book/Online Audio	$24.99

R&B GUITAR
00697356	Book/Online Audio	$19.99
00697433	Songbook/CD Pack	$14.99

ROCK GUITAR
00697319	Book/Online Audio	$16.99
00697383	Songbook/Online Audio	$16.99

ROCKABILLY GUITAR
00697407	Book/Online Audio	$16.99

OTHER METHOD BOOKS

BARITONE GUITAR METHOD
00242055	Book/Online Audio	$12.99

GUITAR FOR KIDS
00865003	Method Book 1/Online Audio	$12.99
00697402	Songbook/Online Audio	$9.99
00128437	Method Book 2/Online Audio	$12.99

MUSIC THEORY FOR GUITARISTS
00695790	Book/Online Audio	$19.99

TENOR GUITAR METHOD
00148330	Book/Online Audio	$12.99

12-STRING GUITAR METHOD
00249528	Book/Online Audio	$19.99

METHOD SUPPLEMENTS

ARPEGGIO FINDER
00697352	6" x 9" Edition	$6.99
00697351	9" x 12" Edition	$9.99

BARRE CHORDS
00697406	Book/Online Audio	$14.99

CHORD, SCALE & ARPEGGIO FINDER
00697410	Book Only	$19.99

GUITAR TECHNIQUES
00697389	Book/Online Audio	$16.99

INCREDIBLE CHORD FINDER
00697200	6" x 9" Edition	$7.99
00697208	9" x 12" Edition	$7.99

INCREDIBLE SCALE FINDER
00695568	6" x 9" Edition	$9.99
00695490	9" x 12" Edition	$9.99

LEAD LICKS
00697345	Book/Online Audio	$10.99

RHYTHM RIFFS
00697346	Book/Online Audio	$14.99

SONGBOOKS

CLASSICAL GUITAR PIECES
00697388	Book/Online Audio	$9.99

EASY POP MELODIES
00697281	Book Only	$7.99
00697440	Book/Online Audio	$14.99

(MORE) EASY POP MELODIES
00697280	Book Only	$6.99
00697269	Book/Online Audio	$14.99

(EVEN MORE) EASY POP MELODIES
00699154	Book Only	$6.99
00697439	Book/Online Audio	$14.99

EASY POP RHYTHMS
00697336	Book Only	$7.99
00697441	Book/Online Audio	$14.99

(MORE) EASY POP RHYTHMS
00697338	Book Only	$7.99
00697322	Book/Online Audio	$14.99

(EVEN MORE) EASY POP RHYTHMS
00697340	Book Only	$7.99
00697323	Book/Online Audio	$14.99

EASY POP CHRISTMAS MELODIES
00697417	Book Only	$9.99
00697416	Book/Online Audio	$14.99

EASY POP CHRISTMAS RHYTHMS
00278177	Book Only	$6.99
00278175	Book/Online Audio	$14.99

EASY SOLO GUITAR PIECES
00110407	Book Only	$9.99

REFERENCE

GUITAR PRACTICE PLANNER
00697401	Book Only	$5.99

GUITAR SETUP & MAINTENANCE
00697427	6" x 9" Edition	$14.99
00697421	9" x 12" Edition	$12.99

For more info, songlists, or to purchase these and more books from your favorite music retailer, go to

halleonard.com

HAL•LEONARD®